"To all the precious people who greet my every visit to Armenia with the words 'Welcome home, James,' and with thanks to God for the home I have found there."

— J.T.

Return Home to Armenia

TUFENKIAN'S ARMENIAN RENAISSANCE

Written by JAMES TUFENKIAN

CARPETS | HOTELS | ECONOMIC DEVELOPMENT
CONSTRUCTION | DESIGN

FOREWORD

Frankly speaking, my birth was an accident. My brother is 16 years older than me, my sister 12. I think my parents were actually kind of surprised that such a thing was possible.

Still, as if to welcome me into the world, Mom recalls holding me up in front of her in the hospital and asking, "Well James, I wonder what God has planned for your life?"

As the answer to that question gradually unfolds, I can say that it has been a pretty interesting ride.

Following is the story of one piece of it. I hope you enjoy it.

—James Tufenkian, New York City

44
58
90
108

Contents

"The Art of Carpet Weaving in the Land of
Armenia is Truly Ancient."

Oushak Collection, TP3 AF33, Navereh Coral

‹‹‹ *An ancient stone church*

MAKING THINGS IN ARMENIA

Historical Background

The first nation to adopt Christianity, in the year 301. Situated at the crossroads of Europe and Asia between the Mediterranean, Caspian, and Black Seas. Eastern outpost of the Byzantine Empire for 800 years. Armenia bore the brunt of each new onslaught of invaders hoping to conquer Byzantium, seize its riches, and extinguish the Christianity that it nurtured and spread throughout Europe. Scythians, Mongols, Arabs, Mamluks, Turks and more ravaged, or were ravaged first in the Anatolian highlands of Armenia.

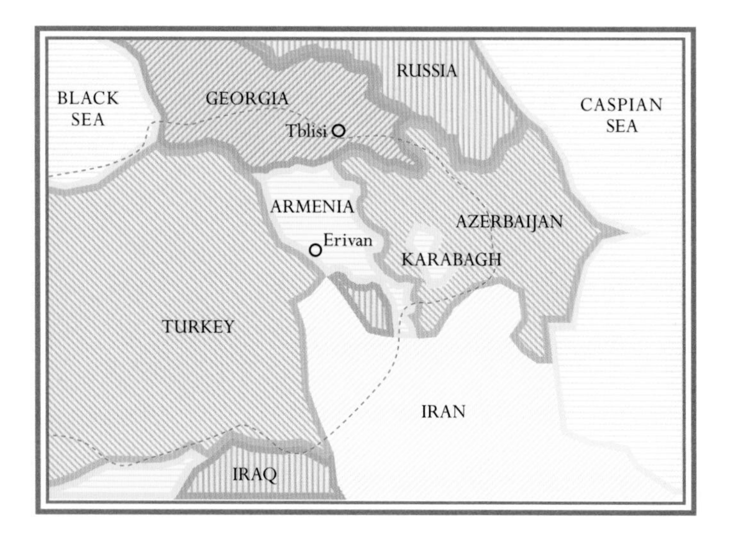

------------------ ANCIENT ARMENIA

Oushak Collection, TP9 AL58, Marand Aqua

Armenia was finally crushed as an independent nation in the 13th century. Its people suffered, and many dispersed to create new communities throughout the world. But somehow Armenians survived for the next 600 years despite the harsh domination of successive Moslem overlords in their land of rugged mountains, austere stone churches and perpetual bloodshed and mourning.

››› *Tufenkian Armenian Carpets, inspired by native colors*

The Caucasus shape the countryside and culture of Armenia

My Story

My grandparents left Turkish Anatolia for America in 1895. In doing so they saved us as a family from a lot of really bad history. The Hamidian Massacres of 1895-96, and the Genocide of 1915 during which Armenians were finally eliminated from their historic homeland. A Republic was still-born in the aftermath of the First World War, was overcome by Bolsheviks only two years later, and absorbed into the new Soviet Union as its tiniest Republic. Then came Stalin, the Second World War, and the devastating earthquake of 1988 that killed 30,000—about 1% of the population. Miraculously, in 1991 Armenia was the first Republic to declare its independence from the Soviet Union. But the joy of freedom collapsed as quickly as did all economic and social order.

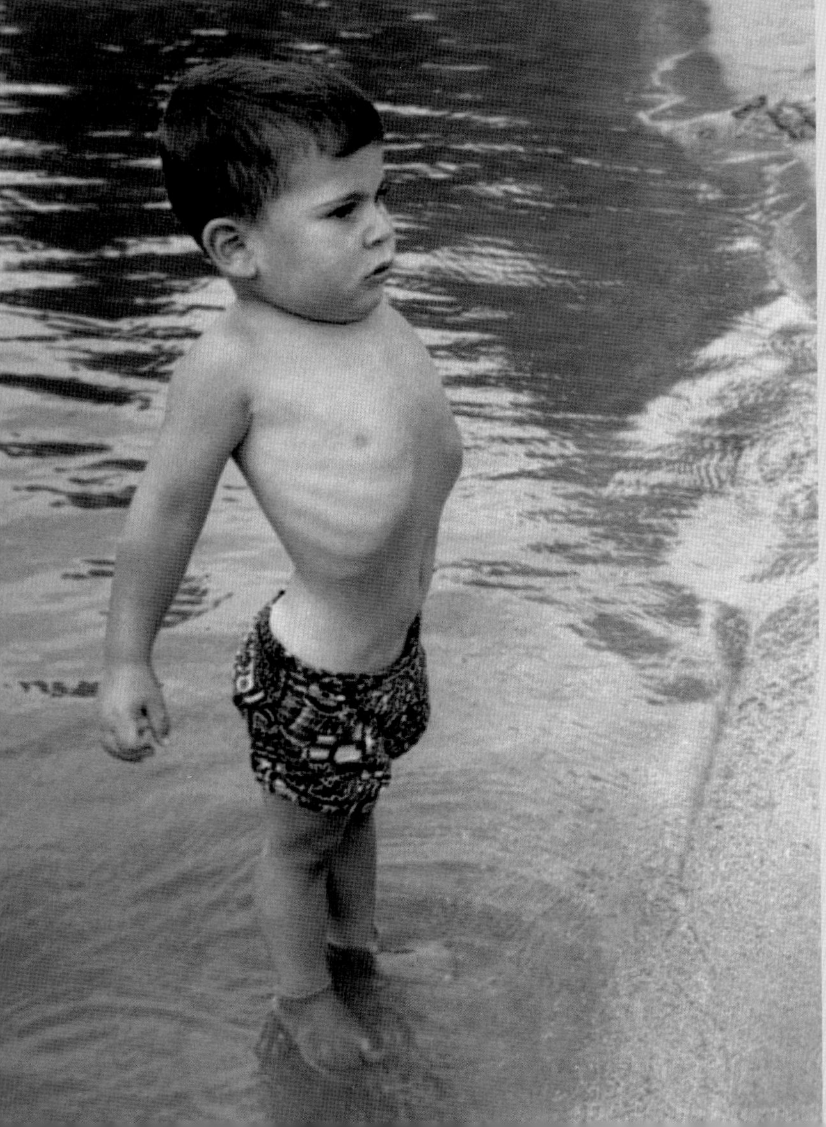

(upper left)

With my sister, mother and brother

(upper right)

Little did I know how happy I was my grandparents emigrated to America`

(left)

Ready to take on the world

I was raised as a white-bread American by parents who revered the values, security, and opportunity of this country. I came late to any awareness of Armenian history and culture. But by 1993 I had created a successful business, and was searching for a cause to fight for. There was no shortage of suffering to alleviate, or causes to support in the world. But as Armenia froze in its second winter without electricity, as people there burnt their furniture and books to generate a little warmth, I started to feel pretty guilty continuing to partake of the 100 years of peace and comfort that resulted from my grandparent's prescient decision to leave. So I decided that out of all the world's causes, I had better start by trying to repay the debt I owed to those who suffered so long during my absence. Off to the land of 1700 year's bad luck.

Tabriz Collection, TAB-4 AS93, Herat Pale Mocha

Tabriz Collection, TAB-3 AT80, Jozan Glacier

››› *Lake Sevan*

Using Business as the Means

My goal in Armenia, as in all my businesses was to:

1. Make beautiful things of enduring value
2. Make a profit from selling them
3. Use that profit and the employment provided to enrich the lives of the workers and their communities.

››› *Hundreds of women, barely surviving on government pensions, now earn a living knitting all wool bed covers.*

Handouts are debilitating in most cases, as we have learned. During the years of Soviet rule Armenia was a prosperous and proud Republic. For its people to be suddenly transformed from educated professionals, to helpless unemployed was at least traumatic. Work, any kind of honest and consistent work was some kind of salvation. I thought I could provide it.

The ancient art of carpet weaving reborn.

'Graphs' guide weavers' hands as they create carpets of enduring beauty and charm.

Tabriz Collection, TAB6 AX1, Julfa Garnet

Carpets

All of my business is based on design, and on expressing it in products made with the finest materials, and traditional hand craftsmanship. Respecting craft, respecting tradition, and pairing them with a contemporary sensibility.

In Armenia, in 1993, I started with what I knew best. Carpets. Armenia had no electricity, and its factories and borders were closed. But it had sheep. Great Caucasus Mountain sheep with long, lustrous wool. And a tradition of great carpet weaving. So my small staff and I created a carpet industry based on Armenian wool, carded and spun by hand into yarn. Based on hand-dyeing of the yarn, and of course hand-knotting of the carpets. We took these traditional crafts and put them into the service of Tufenkian Design, to create richly textured, subtly shaded carpets that contribute spectacularly to modern interiors.

Esfahan Collection

Delicate and refined designs named for the Iranian weaving center and holy city near to which 100,000 Armenians were settled by Shah Abbas in the early 17th century.

‹‹‹ detail *Esfahan, 40/2 AAC128, Jasmine Lapis*

Esfahan

TUFENKIAN ARMENIAN CARPETS | Esfahan | 40/4 AAE130 | Cinnabar Amethyst

TUFENKIAN ARMENIAN CARPETS | Esfahan | 40/4 AAG125 | Cinnabar Linen/Russet

TUFENKIAN ARMENIAN CARPETS | Esfahan | 40/3 AAB107 | Cloudband Moss

TUFENKIAN ARMENIAN CARPETS | Esfahan | 40/2 063 | Jasmine Desert Rose

TUFENKIAN ARMENIAN CARPETS | Esfahan | 40/2 AAC128 | Jasmine Lapis

TUFENKIAN ARMENIAN CARPETS | Esfahan | 40/2 100 | Jasmine Rosehip

TUFENKIAN ARMENIAN CARPETS | Esfahan | 40/1 AAA130 | Satara Blue Smoke

TUFENKIAN ARMENIAN CARPETS | Esfahan | 40/1 AAD103 | Satara Claret

TUFENKIAN ARMENIAN CARPETS | Esfahan | 40/1 099 | Satara Jewel

Tabriz Collection

Elegant and detailed designs inspired by carpets from the Northwestern region of Iran once heavily populated by Armenians, and long one of the great carpet weaving centers of the world.

‹‹‹ detail *Tabriz, TAB3 019, Jozan Black / Sage*

Tabriz

TUFENKIAN ARMENIAN CARPETS | Tabriz | TZ11 141 | Arax Chianti

TUFENKIAN ARMENIAN CARPETS | Tabriz | TAB4 122 | Herat Madder/Gold

TUFENKIAN ARMENIAN CARPETS | Tabriz | TAB4 AS93 | Herat Pale Mocha

TUFENKIAN ARMENIAN CARPETS | Tabriz | TAB4 AQ81 | Herat Soapstone

TUFENKIAN ARMENIAN CARPETS | Tabriz | TAB3 019 | Jozan Black/Sage

TUFENKIAN ARMENIAN CARPETS | Tabriz | TAB3 AF63 | Jozan Camel

TUFENKIAN ARMENIAN CARPETS | Tabriz | TAB3 102 | Jozan Claret/Olive

TUFENKIAN ARMENIAN CARPETS | Tabriz | TAB3 AT80 | Jozan Glacier

TUFENKIAN ARMENIAN CARPETS | Tabriz | TAB3 AB59 | Jozan Golden Sage

TUFENKIAN ARMENIAN CARPETS | Tabriz | TAB3 103 | Jozan Mahogany/Olive

TUFENKIAN ARMENIAN CARPETS | Tabriz | TAB3 AS91 | Jozan Walnut

TUFENKIAN ARMENIAN CARPETS | Tabriz | TAB6 AX1 | Julfa Garnet

TUFENKIAN ARMENIAN CARPETS | Tabriz | TAB6 AW94 | Julfa Mustard Seed

TUFENKIAN ARMENIAN CARPETS | Tabriz | TAB6 100 | Julfa Olive/Mahogany

TUFENKIAN ARMENIAN CARPETS | Tabriz | TAB2 AS92 | Mahabad Basalt

TUFENKIAN ARMENIAN CARPETS | Tabriz | TAB2 019 | Mahabad Black/Claret

TUFENKIAN ARMENIAN CARPETS | Tabriz | TAB2 083 | Mahabad Gravel/Black

TUFENKIAN ARMENIAN CARPETS | Tabriz | TAB2 103 | Mahabad Mahogany/Khaki

TUFENKIAN ARMENIAN CARPETS | Tabriz | TAB2 100 | Mahabad Olive/Mahogany

TUFENKIAN ARMENIAN CARPETS | Tabriz | TAB2 AQ85 | Mahabad Parchment

TUFENKIAN ARMENIAN CARPETS | Tabriz | TAB2 AP16 | Mahabad Ruby

TUFENKIAN ARMENIAN CARPETS | Tabriz | TAB2 AR87 | Mahabad Soapstone

TUFENKIAN ARMENIAN CARPETS | Tabriz | TAB2 AA39 | Mahabad Sunstruck

TUFENKIAN ARMENIAN CARPETS | Tabriz | TZ10 039 | Sephora Pistachio

TUFENKIAN ARMENIAN CARPETS | Tabriz | TAB9 AV85 | Dragon Shore

Powerful and somewhat naïve designs from 19th and early 20th century Anatolia in characteristically pale and warm colors.

‹‹‹ detail *Oushak, TP9 AL58, Marand Aqua*

Oushak

TUFENKIAN ARMENIAN CARPETS | Oushak | TP5 AI8 | Aragats Mist

TUFENKIAN ARMENIAN CARPETS | Oushak | TP4 AH20 | Gharni Barley

TUFENKIAN ARMENIAN CARPETS | Oushak | TP4 AI19 | Gharni Raven

TUFENKIAN ARMENIAN CARPETS | Oushak | TP8 N47 | Gohar Camel

TUFENKIAN ARMENIAN CARPETS | Oushak | TP9 AL58 | Marand Aqua

TUFENKIAN ARMENIAN CARPETS | Oushak | TP9 AI59 | Marand Flagstone

TUFENKIAN ARMENIAN CARPETS | Oushak | TP3 AF33 | Navereh Coral

TUFENKIAN ARMENIAN CARPETS | Oushak | TP3 N59 | Navereh Flagstone

TUFENKIAN ARMENIAN CARPETS | Oushak | TP1 AA62 | Sardarabad Clove

TUFENKIAN ARMENIAN CARPETS | Oushak | TP1 AD49 | Sardarabad Spice

TUFENKIAN ARMENIAN CARPETS | Oushak | TP1 AC63 | Sardarabad Stone

TUFENKIAN ARMENIAN CARPETS | Oushak | TP2 129 | Sebastia Fawn

TUFENKIAN ARMENIAN CARPETS | Oushak | TP2 F46 | Sebastia Golden Sage

Kazak Collection

Bold, archetypal designs executed in vibrant colors from the history of Caucasian Armenian carpet weaving.

‹‹‹ detail *Kazak, A34 T02, Kazakh II Navy*

Kazak

TUFENKIAN ARMENIAN CARPETS | Kazak | A17T48 | Bordjalu Green | 5' x 7'

TUFENKIAN ARMENIAN CARPETS | Kazak | A38T48 | Bordjalu II Green | 5' x 7'

TUFENKIAN ARMENIAN CARPETS | Kazak | A16T04 | Chelaberd Ruby | 5' x 8'

TUFENKIAN ARMENIAN CARPETS | Kazak | A71 T17 | Chondzoresk II Spruce | 5' x 6'

TUFENKIAN ARMENIAN CARPETS | Kazak | A45 T37 | Crab Kazakh Black | 4' x 4'

TUFENKIAN ARMENIAN CARPETS | Kazak | A62T04 | Dragon Ruby | 8' x 10'

TUFENKIAN ARMENIAN CARPETS | Kazak | A60 T48 | Gendge Gul Green | 6' x 8'

TUFENKIAN ARMENIAN CARPETS | Kazak | A41 T04 | Karabagh Lion Ruby | 5' x 6'

TUFENKIAN ARMENIAN CARPETS | Kazak | A58T14 | Karachopf III Red | 5' x 7'

TUFENKIAN ARMENIAN CARPETS | Kazak | A34 T02 | Kazakh II Navy | 5' x 7'

TUFENKIAN ARMENIAN CARPETS | Kazak | A76T14 | Kazak V Red | 5' x 7'

TUFENKIAN ARMENIAN CARPETS | Kazak | A18 T02 | Pinwheel Kazak II Cobalt | 5' x 6'

TUFENKIAN ARMENIAN CARPETS | Kazak | A18T04 | Pinwheel Kazak II Ruby | 5' x 6'

Tufenkian Heritage Hotels

Armenia has a fantastic Alpine countryside. It also has many villages which have somehow retained their pre-industrial character and customs. Tourism is a source of foreign currency, and a potential basis for development of construction, agriculture, transportation, and a variety of related services. Remarkably Armenia had no hotels in the countryside, and guests were required to make long day

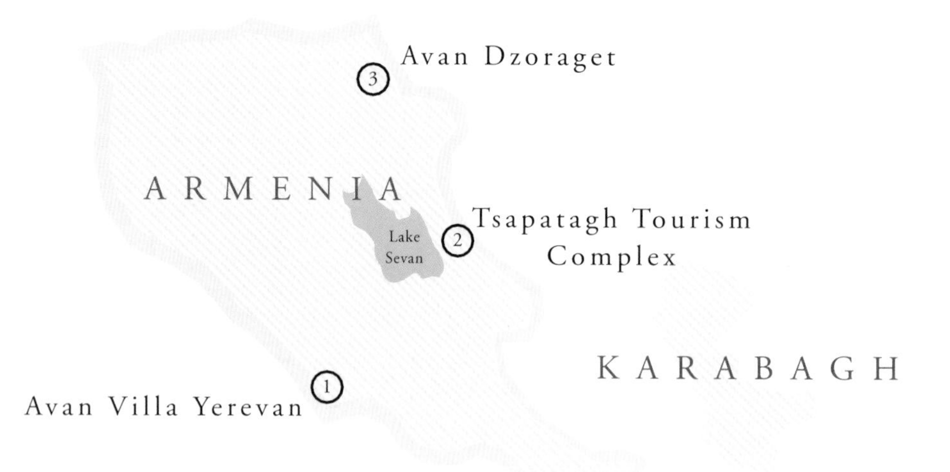

Tufenkian Heritage Hotels are located in some of the most beautiful countryside in Armenia, including (1) Avan Villa Yerevan located on the outskirts of Yerevan, (2) Avan Marak Tsapatagh Hotel located near Lake Sevan and (3) Avan Dzoraget Hotel in the Lori Region.

AVAN VILLA YEREVAN
ԱՎԱՆ ՎԻԼԼԱ ԵՐԵՎԱՆ

HOTEL 1

AVAN VILLA YEREVAN

Located in a peaceful neighborhood 10 minutes from the city center, this luxurious hotel features an environment rich in the design and crafts of a resurgent Armenia.

The private dining room at the Avan Villa Yerevan features an environment crafted with travertine, basalt, wrought iron and wood.

A suite at the Avan Villa Yerevan exhibiting classic design and interiors by traditional Armenian craftsmen. The suite features handmade Tufenkian carpets.

Artist's rendering

HOTEL 2

AVAN MARAK TSAPATAGH AT LAKE SEVAN

Avan Marak Tsapatagh is a mid-priced two floor lodge designed in the style of an old Armenian barn (Marak). In the restaurant Zanazan guests have the opportunity to observe and participate in making traditional Armenian foods. (Open July 2002)

Zanazan Restaurant under construction (artist's rendering)

The first floor of a duplex at the Avan Marak Tsapatagh, featuring furniture and accessories handmade by Armenian craftsmen. (artist's rendering)

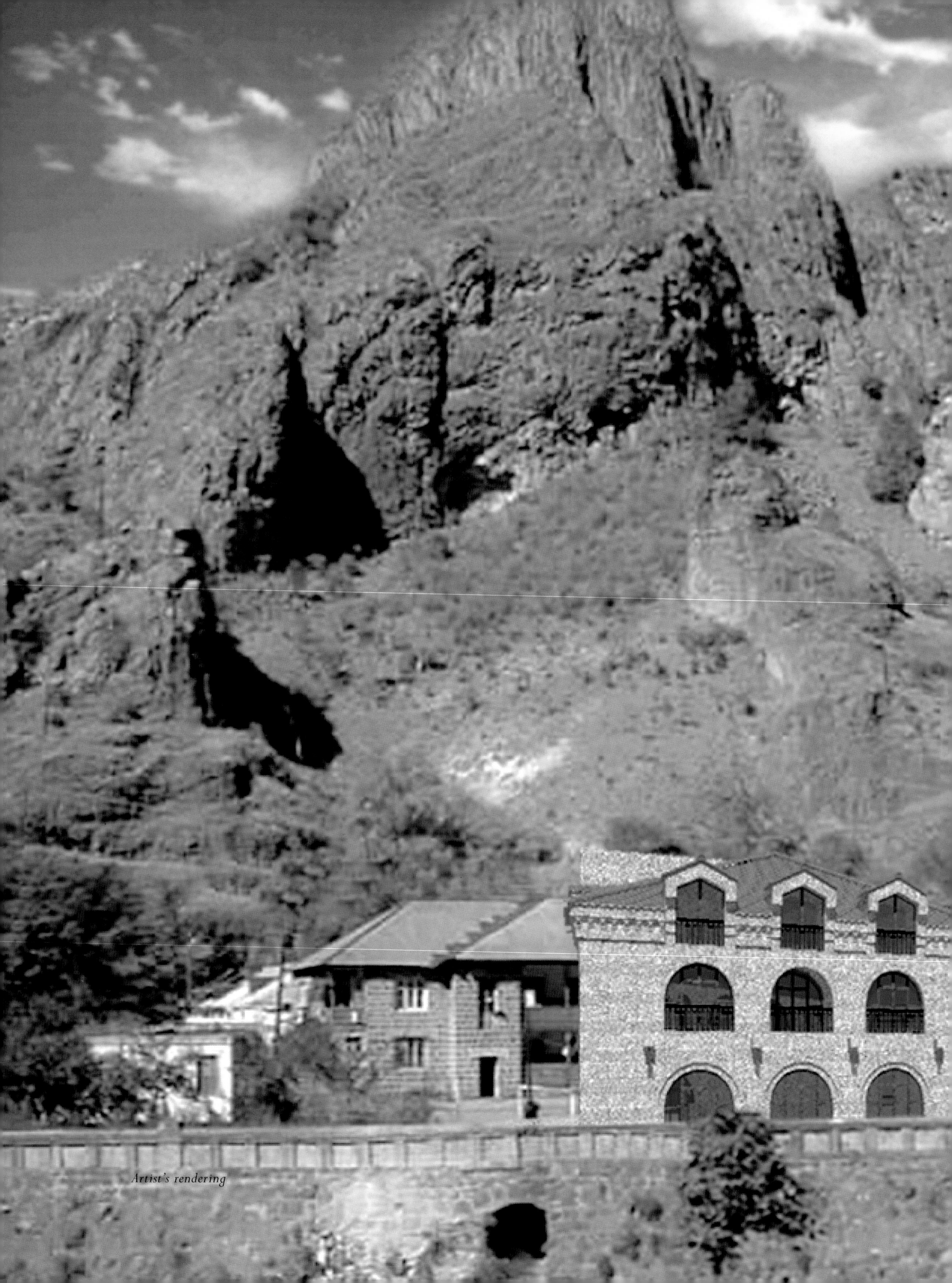
Artist's rendering

HOTEL 3

AVAN DZORAGET IN THE LORI REGION

The Avan Dzoraget Hotel is located alongside the rushing Debed River and surrounded by spectacular rock formations. The Lori Region is a land filled with wonderful mountain landscapes, ruins of medieval fortresses and beautiful monasteries. (Open May 2003)

Restaurant (artist's rendering)

Lobby (artist's rendering)

Main lobby-Avan Villa Yerevan

Balconies adorn the rear of the Avan Villa Yerevan

trips to its many historic and scenic locations from the capital in Yerevan. So it did not take much genius to conceive of Tufenkian Heritage Hotels. Initially 3 sites in construction in the main regions of the country. Each located within a scenic and historic village setting. Each a part of the village, the guest

The restaurant features locally crafted tables, chairs and chandeliers

experience enriched by the food, crafts, customs and rhythm of daily village life, as well as the natural beauty, outdoor activities, and historical sites of the region. Each a base for economic development of the resources of its region.

For more information visit us on the web at www.tufenkian.am

"Armenia has many villages which have somehow retained their pre-industrial character and customs."

– James Tufenkian

Construction

I love stone. Not surprisingly. Solid. Permanent. Textured. Primal. And I love the craftsmanship and the craftsmen who create structures from stone so finely shaped that when completed, it seems to have been composed of a solid sheet. Armenia is a land of stone and stone masons. A land of massive walls in massive structures. Basalt, Tufa, Travertine and Marble. I was drawn to build in Armenia. Inevitably. Hypnotically.

Esfahan Collection, 40/3 AAB107, Cloudband Moss

Tufenkian Design

Design is inseparable from craft and material for me. I am uninterested in ornament. I like to reduce things to their essence. That essence is the color and texture of the natural materials used to create them. It is the traditional craftsmanship by which they are made, and the human touch that enlivens them in so many subtle ways. With fine materials, and traditional crafts I try to create interior items and environments that are serene and comfortable, and which yet somehow stir the imagination.

Iron chair

Nightstand

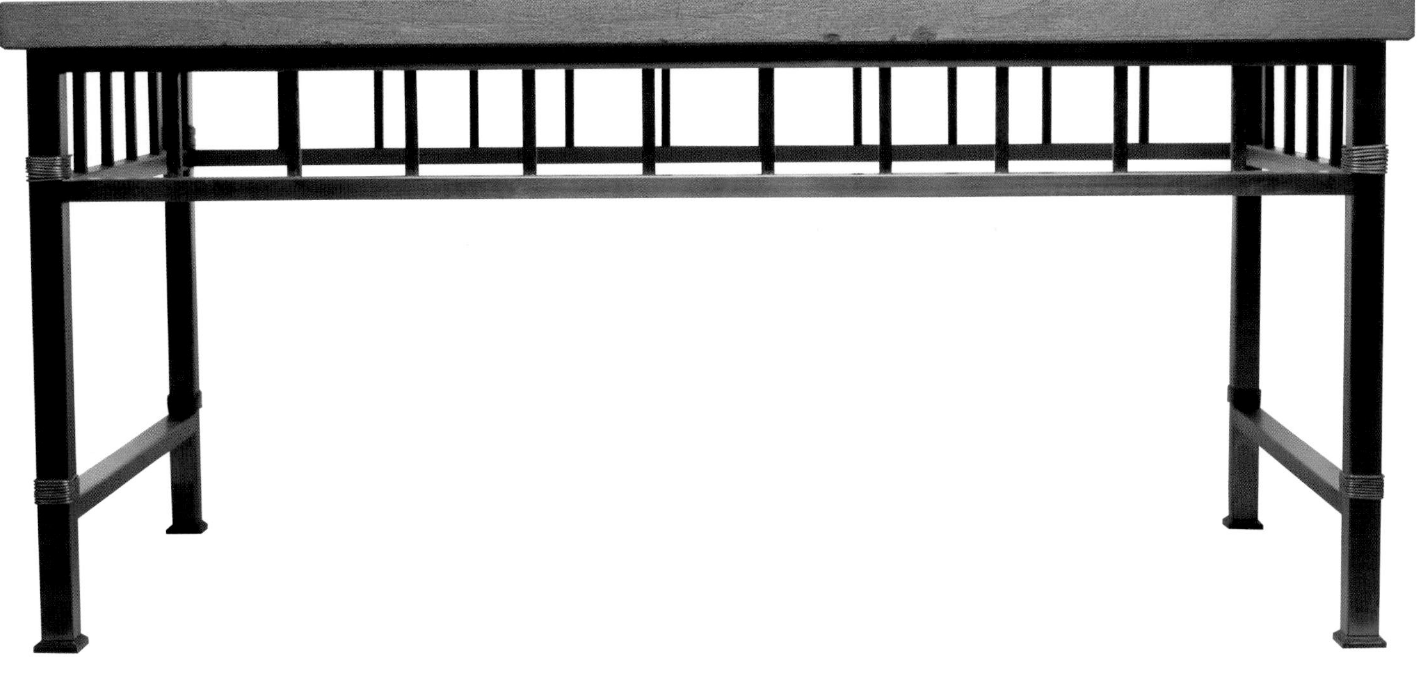

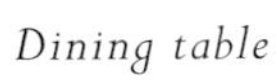

Dining table

The Armenian Knitting Ladies

The suffering of really decent people really kills me. All around the world you find people with skills, energy and desire, completely stymied and frustrated. Forced to idly wait through their days. Starving slowly in flesh and in spirit. I try not to look. To acknowledge this reality only occasionally, only briefly. The Armenian Knitting Ladies was one chance I had to magically combine great skill, great creativity, great materials and terrible suffering into a project where everyone participates, and everyone wins. The knitters. The company. The consumer. And I can sleep a little better.

››› *The reward for Maria's work is a regular income that she says is a "gift from God."*

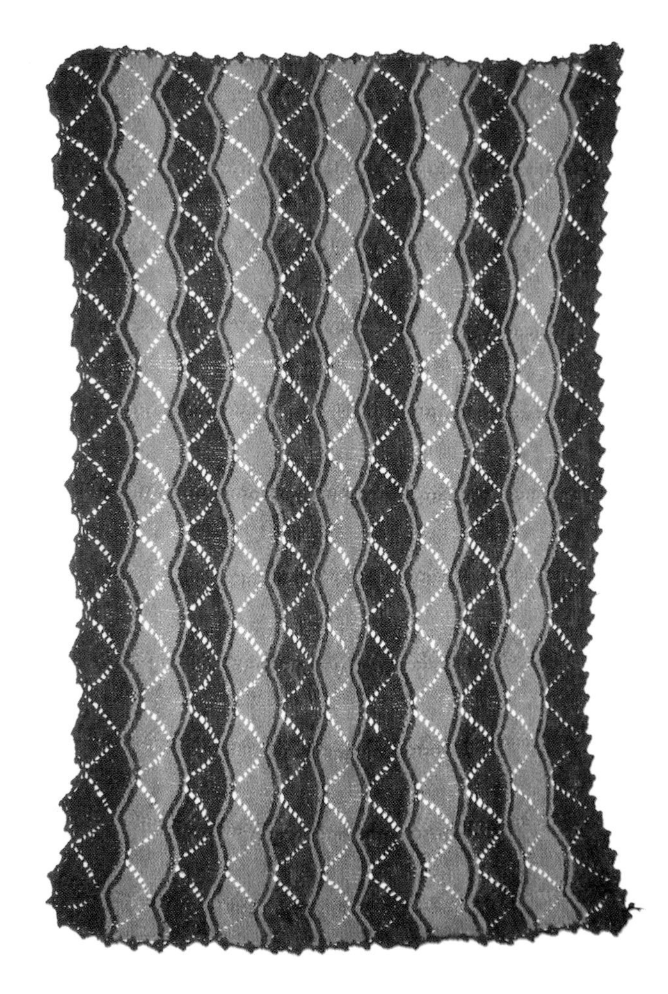

The Tufenkian Foundation

The Foundation aims to create sustainable projects that enrich the beneficiaries spiritually, as well as physically. If we ever handout it is with great care and forethought, and where there is no choice. As a small Foundation in a world of giant "benevolents," and even larger problems, we try to make a little go a long way by cleverly planning for each of our actions to ripple through multiple layers of the needy.

So one project pays the employable poor to make food, clothing, and household necessities. These are distributed by volunteers of all classes who just love the satisfaction of helping. The final beneficiaries are the elderly or handicapped who are unable to help themselves.

The Jil Sheep Farm

In another, we buy lambs from poor countryside farmers, creating herds of 500 sheep. The sheep are then loaned to hopeless refugees who volunteer to resettle abandoned villages. The annual shearing of the sheep is bought by the Tufenkian carpet manufacturing company for its production. In addition, extra lambs and the milk from the ewes are sold in the market providing an economic base for the village. Each year part of the growth in the herd is repaid to the Foundation, and used to settle new villages.

We are forming corps of unemployed to clean up the common areas of residential buildings and gardens ignored by residents who are still waiting for the Soviet to take care. Once the volunteers start, the residents feel compelled to join in, and a new consciousness of self-help is created.

We have funded a radio station that will broadcast spiritual and classical music in a market where there is only Russian pop and American rock to be heard. The idea is to uplift the local population with music on a higher plane. The programming consists largely of recordings made in Armenia, and performed by local artists who are supported and encouraged by the opportunity. Discussion shows are planned to reawaken interest in social issues and social action.

Overall our aims are modest. We hope that our efforts can increase at least a little faster than the need for them.

Children at an orphanage funded by The Tufenkian Foundation

Local artisans are supported by the Foundation

Our People

My small staff and I created a carpet industry based on Armenian wool—carded, spun, knotted and dyed, all by hand. We took these traditional hand crafts and put them into the service of Tufenkian Design, to create richly textured, subtly shaded carpets that contribute spectacularly to modern interiors.

— James Tufenkian

Edgar Janjutyan
Sales Manager

Lusine Bagiryan
Office Manager

Erick Naikian
Procurement Manager

Anahit Avetisyan
Finance Manager

James Tufenkian
President

Garik Chilingarian
General Manager

Anna Ghalechyan
Executive Assistant to the President

Gurgen Kostanyan
Chief Accountant

Lilit Hakobyan
Public Relations Manager

Tigran Ghazaryan
Marketing Manager

Tevos Eghiazaryan
Manager of Production

Elmira Eghiazaryan
Chief of Laboratory

Evgenia Shahbazyan
Manager of Dyeing Department

Mileta Vardanyan
Chief Painter

Alla Vardanyan
Painter

Gevorg Safaryan
Chief Accountant

Hayk Safaryan
Deputy Manager

Neli Manukyan
Office Manager,
Production Manager

Meruzh Karapetyan
Driver, Chief of the Warehouse

Zara Tumanyan
Architect

David Sargsyan
Designer

Hovik Poghosyan
Manager of Documentation

Armen Hovhannisyan
Chief Engineer

Hayk Shatveryan
Deputy Director Construction

Surik Hakobyan
Construction Manager

Tigran Manukyan
Supplier

Gohar Araratyan
Assistant Hotel Manager

Hakob Hakobyan
Hotel Manager

Minas Ervenyan
Head Chef

David Zakaryan
Tufenkian Foundation
Accountant

Hakob Hovhannisyan
Tufenkian Foundation
"Our Duty To Live"
Project Coordinator

Margaret Hovhannisyan
Tufenkian Foundation
Manager, Yerevan

Vardan Tovmasyan
Assistant to Project Coordinator

Samvel Gevorgyan
"Sheep from Farm"
Project Coordinator

THE HISTORY OF CARPET WEAVING IN ARMENIA

The art of carpet weaving in the land of Armenia is truly ancient. No one really knows for sure, but there is good reason to believe that the art originated there. In any case, it is clear that until about four hundred years ago Armenian carpet weaving was preeminent in the world, and was generally recognized as being so.

Marco Polo, the famous world traveler who must have seen many carpets, was one of the many admirers of Armenian carpets. In his thirteenth century account of travels through ancient Armenia, he observed that it was among the Greeks and Armenians "where the best and most beautiful carpets are produced, as well as silk of crimson and other splendid colors."

Perhaps we shouldn't be surprised by Polo's comments. There is evidence, after all, that carpet weaving in the area of ancient Armenia was already a refined art five centuries *before* the birth of Christ. In 1949 archeologists discovered the oldest intact carpet known today in a royal tomb hidden in the Altai Mountains of Mongolia. Amazingly, the Pazyryk Carpet, as it is called, is not the rough and primitive product of an early society. It is instead considered to be finely knotted and highly evolved, even by today's standards.

European scholars have argued convincingly that the origin of the Pazyryk Carpet was in pre-Armenian Urartu, based on its design elements which are documented in surviving Urartian monuments, and in its depiction of Hittite dress and horse ornaments. Analysis of the red dyes used in the carpet show that they originated in the Ararat plain where they were recognized for thousands of years as an exclusive product of the region.

Armenian carpets were traded to the corners of the known world, but they reached their extraordinary level of development because they were an essential part of the fabric of Armenian life. Armenian sources refer to carpets being used to adorn the floors and walls from churches beginning in the fifth century, and describe sumptuous meals consumed while seated on these carpets.

Records, literature, and historical accounts from Greek, Roman, Persian, Arab, Bulgarian and other sources mention Armenian carpets given in tribute, paid as taxes, or taken as booty, beginning in pre-Christian times. Surprisingly, Arab sources acknowledge the supremacy of Christian Armenian prayer rugs, even though these rugs are often thought of as the quintessential Islamic art form. What is also remarkable from historical accounts is that the Armenian carpets were not merely the small products of home looms, but were the result of organized commercial enterprises that created huge works of exceptional beauty. A single carpet sometimes covered as much as 60 square meters.

All of this began to change, as did the association of Armenians with the weaving of great carpets, when the Armenian kingdom of Cilicia fell in AD 1375. At that time many Armenians fled their homeland and settled in Egypt, Transylvania, Poland, and Persia. Not coincidentally, it was during this time that carpet weaving became prominent among the Mamluks of Egypt and in the other regions where Armenians settled. They carried their craft with them and transferred it to the populations of their host countries.

At the beginning of the seventeenth century, the Persian Shah Abbas transplanted 100,000 Armenians from their homes in Julfa, which is in modern Nakhijevan, to New Julfa, constructed outside of the holy city of Isfahan in Persia. He gave them a monopoly on the silk trade, sending them to India where they created flourishing commercial outposts. It is from this time that the greatest carpets of Persia and Moghul India were created. At the same time, the famous Polish court carpets known as Polonaise were woven in Isfahan, and presented to the royalty of Poland which, by then, had a thriving community of more than 100,000 Armenians.

Great carpet weaving followed the Armenians wherever they settled but, unfortunately, the Armenian contribution to weaving was obscured. Armenians, a people without a country, came to be known as merely the traders who brought the carpets of their adoptive lands to the corners of the world. During the past several centuries, Armenians have mainly been identified with the great carpets of the Caucasus, despite their undeniable contribution in creating the much-admired Oushak carpets of Anatolia, and the Tabriz carpets of northwestern Iran.

Armenian carpets from the Caucasus are as magnificent as they are diverse. Early on, the bold Dragon carpets of the seventeenth century were created. Later, beginning in the early nineteenth century, came the French-influenced floral carpets that were made in Nagorno Karabagh for members of the Russian aristocracy. Prized by collectors for the past century, Armenian Caucasian carpets are characterized by their powerful and inspired designs, their brilliant colors, and their velvety wool pile.

During Soviet times the cottage industry of carpet weaving practiced by most Armenian women of the time was slowly strangled. Individual enterprise was discouraged, and the carpet industry was centralized into a monolithic state organization that monopolized the craft. Not surprisingly, Soviet values emphasized quantity and conformity over passion and creativity, which was devastating to the continuation of the lively folk art tradition of carpet weaving. Consequently, most of the Soviet-era carpets are as bland and uninspired as the workplaces in which they were created.

Fortunately, with the fall of the Soviet system and the independence of Armenia, there is now a movement underway to revive the artistry of ancient Armenian carpet making. Paramount are the old values—use of the best indigenous Caucasian mountain wool, yarn brushed and spun entirely by hand, and colors inspired by the great carpets of the past.

Once again, beautiful carpets with integrity and spirit are being created in Armenia, commanding high prices and great respect in the markets of Europe and North America. In the process, thousands of people are proudly employed in the revival of this truly Armenian art form.

Design Coordinates

ARMENIAN COORDINATES

DESIGN/ COLOR CODE	DESIGN / COLOR NAME	ARMENIAN COORDINATE #1	ARMENIAN COORDINATE #2	ARMENIAN COORDINATE #3
TP5/AI8	Aragats Mist	Gharni Raven	Jozan Black/Sage	Marand Flagstone
TZ11/AA62	Arax Chianti	Jozan Mahogany/ Olive	Julfa Olive/ Mahogany	Mahabad Olive/ Mahogany
40/4/AAE130	Cinnabar Amethyst	Satara Blue Smoke	Jasmine Lapis	
40/4/AAG125	Cinnabar Linen Russet	Satara Claret		
40/3/AAB107	Cloudband Moss	Satara Blue Smoke	Jozan Glacier	
TAB4/AV85	Dragon Shore	Herat Soapstone	Mahabad Parchment	
TP4/AH20	Gharni Barley	Sebastia Fawn	Mahabad Sunstruck	
TP4/AI19	Gharni Raven	Aragats Mist	Jozan Black/Sage	
TP8/N47	Gohar Camel	Navereh Flagstone	Jozan Golden Sage	Julfa Mustard Seed
TAB4/AS93	Herat Madder/ Gold	Julfa Garnet	Jasmine Desert Rose	
TAB4/122	Herat Pale Mocha	Mahabad Basalt	Sephora Pistachio	Herat Soapstone
TAB4/AQ81	Herat Soapstone	Mahabad Soapstone	Jozan Walnut	Herat Pale Mocha
40/2/63	Jasmine Desert Rose	Jasmine Rosehip	Satara Jewel	
40/2/AAC128	Jasmine Lapis	Satara Blue Smoke	Cinnabar Amethyst	
40/2/100	Jasmine Rosehip	Satara Jewel	Jasmine Desert Rose	
TAB3/19	Jozan Black/ Sage	Marand Flagstone	Gharni Raven	
TAB3/AF63	Jozan Camel	Sardarabad Spice	Navereh Coral	
TAB3/102	Jozan Claret/ Olive	Julfa Olive/ Mahogany	Mahabad Olive/Mahogany	
TAB3/AT80	Jozan Glacier	Marand Aqua	Dragon Shore	
TAB3/AB59	Jozan Golden/ Sage	Sardarabad Stone	Navereh Flagstone	
TAB3/103	Jozan Mahogany/ Olive	Julfa Olive/ Mahogany	Mahabad Mahogany/ Khaki	Mahabad Olive/Mahogany
TAB3/AS91	Jozan Walnut	Herat Pale Mocha	Marand Aqua	Mahabad Parchment
TAB6/AX1	Julfa Garnet	Herat Madder/Gold	Satara Jewel	
TAB4/AW94	Julfa Mustard Seed	Gohar Camel	Navereh Flagstone	
TAB4/100	Julfa Olive/ Mahogany	Jozan Mahogany/ Olive	Mahabad Olive/Mahogany	Arax Chianti
TAB2/AS92	Mahabad Basalt	Herat Soapstone	Mahabad Parchment	Sephora Pistachio
TAB2/19	Mahabad Black Claret	Mahabad Gravel/ Black		
TAB2/83	Mahabad Gravel/ Black	Mahabad Black/ Claret		
TAB2/103	Mahabad Mahogany/ Khaki	Jozan Mahogany/Olive	Mahabad Olive/Mahogany	
TAB2/100	Mahabad Olive/ Mahogany	Julfa Olive/ Mahogany	Mahabad Mahogany/Khaki	Jozan Mahogany /Olive
TAB2/AQ85	Mahabad Parchment	Mahabad Basalt	Sephora Pistachio	
TAB2/AP16	Mahabad Ruby	Jasmine Desert Rose		
TAB2/AR87	Mahabad Soapstone	Herat Soapstone	Jozan Glacier	Cloudband Moss
TAB2/AA39	Mahabad Sunstruck	Sardarabad Clove	Sephora Pistachio	
TP9/AL58	Marand Aqua	Jozan Glacier	Julfa Mustard Seed	Herat Soapstone
TP9/AI59	Marand Flagstone	Gharni Raven	Jozan Black/Sage	Aragats Mist
TP3/AF33	Navereh Coral	Sardarabad Spice	Jozan Camel	Jozan Golden Sage
TP3/N59	Navereh Flagstone	Gohar Camel	Jozan Golden Sage	Julfa Mustard Seed
TP1/AA62	Sardarabad Clove	Jozan Golden Sage	Mahabad Sunstruck	
TP1/AD49	Sardarabad Spice	Jozan Camel	Navereh Coral	
TP1/AC63	Sardarabad Stone	Jozan Golden Sage	Julfa Mustard Seed	
40/1/AAA130	Satara Blue Smoke	Cloudband Moss	Cinnabar Amethyst	Jasmine Lapis
40/1/AAD103	Satara Claret	Cinnabar Linen/Russet		
40/1/99	Satara Jewel	Jasmine Desert Rose	Jasmine Rosehip	Julfa Garnet
TP2/I29	Sebastia Fawn	Mahabad Sunstruck	Sephora Pistachio	
TP2/F46	Sebastia Golden Sage	Jozan Golden Sage	Gharni Barley	Julfa Mustard Seed
TZ10/39	Sephora Pistachio	Julfa Mustard Seed	Gohar Camel	Mahabad Sunstruck

ARMENIAN WITH TIBETAN FULL LINE COORDINATES

DESIGN/ COLOR CODE	DESIGN / COLOR NAME	FULL LINE COORDINATE #1	FULL LINE COORDINATE #2	FULL LINE COORDINATE #3
TP5/AI8	Aragats Mist	Arak Black	Polonaise Cloisonne	Bidjar Black
TZ11/AA62	Arax Chianti	Zeytoun Mahogany / Avocado	Zenjan Caviar	Zagros Brick
40/4/AAE130	Cinnabar Amethyst	Kyoto Mauve Sky	Eclipse Blue/Mauve	Cave Culture Blue/ Mauve
40/4/AAG125	Cinnabar Linen Russet	Zagros Rock/ Spruce		
40/3/AAB107	Cloudband Moss	Kensington Artichoke	Zeytoun Cove	Interlocking Squares Aloe
TAB4/AV85	Dragon Shore	Chimera Mineral	Zeytoun Cove	
TP4/AH20	Gharni Barley	Zahrani Gilt	Chimera Lemongrass	
TP4/AI19	Gharni Raven	Arak Black	Karadjah Burlap	Bidjar Black
TP8/N47	Gohar Camel	Floral Heriz Corn	Mahal Ivory	Zeytoun Dawn
TAB4/AS93	Herat Madder/ Gold	Erzerum Umber/Ruby	Kensington Paprika	Chimera Bouquet
TAB4/122	Herat Pale Mocha	Arak Sand	Zeytoun Cove	Afshan Pale Taupe
TAB4/AQ81	Herat Soapstone	Afshan Pale Taupe	Arak Moss	Bidjar Ambergris
40/2/63	Jasmine Desert Rose	Kensington Paprika	Tumbledown Mixed Pallet	
40/2/AAC128	Jasmine Lapis	Shajahan Wildflower Blue	Zeytoun Cove	
40/2/100	Jasmine Rosehip	Bidjar Sandalwood	Checkerboard Mahogany/ Curry	Mahal Tobacco/ Moss
TAB3/19	Jozan Black/ Sage	Polonaise Cloisonne	Cathedral Coal	Bidjar Black
TAB3/AF63	Jozan Camel	Zahrani Gilt	Bidjar Sunswept	Agra Border Honey
TAB3/102	Jozan Claret/ Olive	Zeytoun Mahogany Avocado	Zagros Musk	Snakes & Ladders Morrocan Red
TAB3/AT80	Jozan Glacier	Zagros II Sea Amber	Kensington Artichoke	
TAB3/AB59	Jozan Golden/ Sage	Arak Sand	Cathedral Pale Yellow	Critter Prints Moss
TAB3/103	Jozan Mahogany/ Olive	Zeytoun Mahogany Avocado	Marash Ruby	
TAB3/AS91	Jozan Walnut	Zeytoun Cove	Shajahan Wildflower Blue	Kensington Artichoke
TAB6/AX1	Julfa Garnet	Zeytoun Mahogany Avocado		
TAB4/AW94	Julfa Mustard Seed	Afshan Sage	Afshan Pale Taupe	
TAB4/100	Julfa Olive/ Mahogany	Shajahan Ruby		
TAB2/AS92	Mahabad Basalt	Arak Sand	Zeytoun Cove	Afshan Pale Taupe
TAB2/19	Mahabad Black Claret	Zenjan Mahogany	Ferns Black Velvet	Zenjan Caviar
TAB2/83	Mahabad Gravel/ Black	Zenjan Caviar	Ferns Black Velvet	
TAB2/103	Mahabad Mahogany/ Khaki	Zeytoun Mahogany/Avocado	Marsh Ruby	Screen Mahogany
TAB2/100	Mahabad Olive/ Mahogany	Zagros Musk	Zeytoun Mahogany/Avocado	Marash Ruby
TAB2/AQ85	Mahabad Parchment	Afshan Pale Taupe	Arak Sand	Kensington Artichoke
TAB2/AP16	Mahabad Ruby	Erzerum Umber/Ruby	Shajahan Ruby	Bidjar Sandalwood
TAB2/AR87	Mahabad Soapstone	Zeytoun Cove	Afshan Pale Taupe	
TAB2/AA39	Mahabad Sunstruck	Floral Heriz Corn	Zahrani Gilt	
TP9/AL58	Marand Aqua	Donegal Branches Winter	Zeytoun Cove	Zagros Sea Amber
TP9/AI59	Marand Flagstone	Polonaise Cloisonne	Cathedral Moss	Afshan Sage
TP3/AF33	Navereh Coral	Floral Heriz Clay	Agra Border Honey	Donegal II Salamander
TP3/N59	Navereh Flagstone	Floral Heriz Corn	Mahal Ivory	Zeytoun Dawn
TP1/AA62	Sardarabad Clove	Mahal Ivory	Marash Straw	Bidjar Sunswept
TP1/AD49	Sardarabad Spice	Zagros Ecru	Bidjar Salmonberry	
TP1/AC63	Sardarabad Stone	Bidjar Sunswept	Afshan Sage	
40/1/AAA130	Satara Blue Smoke	Eclipse Blue/Mauve	Kyoto Mauve Sky	Go Green Ice
40/1/AAD103	Satara Claret	Chimera Purple Haze	Kyoto Mauve Sky	
40/1/99	Satara Jewel	Zenjan Mahogany	Zenjan Caviar	Bidjar Sandalwood
TP2/I29	Sebastia Fawn	Bidjar Sunswept	Zahrani Gilt	Argyle Caramel
TP2/F46	Sebastia Golden Sage	Argyle Caramel	Cathedral Pale Yellow	
TZ10/39	Sephora Pistachio	Bidjar Ambergris	Shajahan Castle	Mahal Ivory

Armenian Craft Items

Ironwork

BALCONY/GARDEN CHAIRS
These hand-forged chairs are surprisingly light and delicate.

BARBEQUE SET
Includes nine implements that can be hung from a wall mounted rack. The handles are reminiscent of the hilt of a medieval knight's sword.

BATHROOM MIRROR
The frame is made of iron and includes a marble sill.

CHANDELIERS
The chandelier has ten lamps that are affixed to "arms" that have been forged into the shape of leaves.

CURTAIN HOLDERS
On either end of the curtain rod there are two pear-shaped 'balls.'

DRAGON TABLE
The Dragon table gets its name from Dragon heads that are affixed to two sides of the branches that emerge from the single support.

DINING TABLE
A modern design incorporating a metal top and iron legs.

Balcony/Garden Chairs

Chandeliers

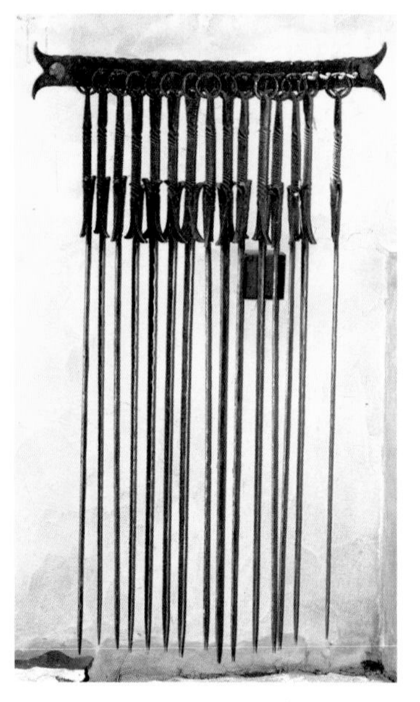

Barbeque Set

Curtain Holders

Dragon Table

Bathroom Mirror

Dining Table

Native Crafts, Native Materials

Fireplace Set

Headboard

Iron Chair

Nightstand Lamp

Trashcan

FIREPLACE SET

Made of iron, the set can be attached to a wall. It has three elements: two pokers, a brush and a dustpan.

HEADBOARD

Headboards are made in three sizes—small, medium and large. Each includes small bars made of iron, with brass accents.

IRON CHAIR

This incredibly comfortable chair is specially designed to provide lumbar support for the lower back.

NIGHTSTAND LAMP

The base of the lamp is made of marble. Three iron posts are set in the base, one supports the lampshade, the others are decorative.

TRASHCAN

The trashcan is made of one piece of iron decorated with yellow iron 'dots' that give it a magical look.

Woodworking

BALCONY TABLE
A chic table whose legs descend from the surface like waves, instead of the usual straight legs. (not shown)

CLOSET
This wardrobe is simply designed, made from flat sheets of walnut.

LUGGAGE RACK
Actually a small table with hand-made carpet attached to its surface with an angular iron frame.

MAFRASH-COVERED BENCH
This oaken bench was historically used as both a bench and table.

Stone

COFFEE TABLE
Metal bars and brass compliment the table's untilled basalt stone top. (not shown)

STONE-CAPPED DESK
This desk's untilled gray basalt top gives the impression of ancient times.

STONE-CAPPED NIGHTSTAND
Untilled basalt stone tops a book-shelf and four metal legs indented from the top.

Closet

Luggage Rack

Mafrash-Covered Bench

Stone-Capped Desk

Stone-Capped Nightstand

Cover Photograph and photographs of Armenia
© Matthew Karanian and Robert Kurkjian
Stone Garden Productions
4501 Connecticut Avenue, Suite 1112
Washington DC, USA
Photographs of the interiors © 1998-2002 Stewart O'Shields
Photographs of the carpets © 1997-2002 Alec Hemer

Production coordinator: Mark DaSilva
Design and print production: Dan Miller Design, New York
Printed and bound in Hong Kong

ISBN 0-9677509-2-X

Tufenkian Carpets
902 Broadway
New York, New York 10010
Websites www.tufenkiancarpets.com www.tufenkian.am

Although every effort has been made to faithfully reproduce rug colors, due to the natural variation in the production of both our rugs and printed materials, we recommend visiting a Tufenkian dealer to view our rugs.

For further information, or to locate the nearest Tufenkian dealer, call 1-800-475-4788 or visit us on the web at www.tufenkiancarpets.com or www.tufenkian.am